# THE PORTAGE POETRY SERIES

*Fulgurite*
Catherine Kyle

*The Body Is Burden and Delight*
Sharon White

*Bone Country*
Linda Nemec Foster

*Not Just the Fire*
R.B. Simon

*Monarch*
Heather Bourbeau

*The Walk to Cefalù*
Lynne Viti

*The Found Object Imagines a Life: New and Selected Poems*
Mary Catherine Harper

*Naming the Ghost*
Emily Hockaday

*Mourning*
Dokubo Melford Goodhead

*Messengers of the Gods: New and Selected Poems*
Kathryn Gahl

*After the 8-Ball*
Colleen Alles

*Careful Cartography*
Devon Bohm

*Broken On the Wheel*
Barbara Costas-Biggs

*Sparks and Disperses*
Cathleen Cohen

"The poems in the accomplished 12th book from Foster (*Amber Necklace from Gdansk*) cohere in their lyric commitment to 'that idea of blue. The expanse of the landscape that can't/ be contained in a single image.' These poems range widely in their settings, from Dresden to Detroit, Krakow to Hawaii. Blue sky, blue damask, and 'the blue divide' of ocean that separates North America from Europe refract in a glimpse of the poet's own mother, 'Her blue eyes swimming in the immigrant's/ version of hide and seek,' as the woman washes 'the blue/ of heaven until it shines like a word/ that has yet to be invented.' In other entries, works by Italian masters and contemporary artists come alive through vivid descriptions of color and texture, as does 'a faceless socialist/ painting Sobieski's palace frescoes/ by number.' For Foster, words themselves are a tangible medium, variously inflected, misheard, and treasured: 'Language of bark, leaves, stones, mud;/ of fog sleeping in the marshes and sun caught/ in tangled branches. Language of amber/ sinking into its inclusions and rain falling/ from its clouds.' Rich with closely observed detail, narrative depth, and poignant historical reflections, this is a generous and beautiful collection."

—*Publishers Weekly*

"In *The Blue Divide*, Linda Nemec Foster navigates the edges and depths of worlds both here and beyond…to map what flows between us. Testimonial to human endurance and love song to the human spirit, this gem of a book, retrieved from the deep by a poet at the height of her prowess, is as wide as a 'cavalcade of blue sky' and as deep as 'the blue damask of morning.' Hold these poems up to the light to see the wide blue world (and the world in you) changed, for good."

—Robert Fanning
author of *Severance*

"With clarity and intensity, Linda Nemec Foster dives deep into the shadows, and deep into the light—global landscape, personal touch; faith and art; the sensual and the cruel; forward and backward through generations of family, acknowledging loss wherever it occurs—all with her trademark tenderness and resilience."

—Jim Daniels
author of *Gun/Shy* and *The Middle Ages*

"Both a tourist and an inhabitant everywhere: whether in Warsaw, Cleveland, Sarajevo, New York City, Geneva, Poughkeepsie, Oahu, or Ypsilanti, Linda Nemec Foster finds the stuff of poetry and makes it real and tangible. From 'the thin line of horizon,' she reminds us that 'everything/everything is connected. Whether/we can dare to believe it or not.'"

—Laurel Blossom
author of *Longevity* and *Degrees of Latitude*

"I love the restlessness…the urgency of the poems in *The Blue Divide*, and their deep seriousness—how they peer into the present through layers of history, and peer into history through the lens of the personal; how they're on intimate terms with both public and private violence—and can we tell the difference, after all? Tender, brutal, unflinching, magical—these poems [are] infused with the holiness of the real and the mystery of transcendence: 'face becoming blossom becoming starburst becoming sea.'"

—Cecilia Woloch
author of *Carpathia* and *Earth*

# The Blue Divide

## Poems

## Linda Nemec Foster

CORNERSTONE PRESS
UNIVERSITY OF WISCONSIN-STEVENS POINT

Cornerstone Press, Stevens Point, Wisconsin 54481
Copyright © 2024 Linda Nemec Foster
www.uwsp.edu/cornerstone

Printed in the United States of America by
Point Print and Design Studio, Stevens Point, Wisconsin

Library of Congress Control Number: 2020940715
ISBN: 978-1-960329-29-5 (2nd Ed. Pbk)

First Edition originally published by New Issues Press, 2021.

Cornerstone Press titles are produced in courses and internships offered by the
Department of English at the University of Wisconsin–Stevens Point.

DIRECTOR & PUBLISHER
Dr. Ross K. Tangedal

EXECUTIVE EDITOR
Jeff Snowbarger, Freesia McKee

EDITORIAL DIRECTOR
Ellie Atkinson

SENIOR EDITOR
Brett Hill, Grace Dahl

PRESS STAFF
Carolyn Czerwinski, Sophie McPherson, Natalie Reiter, Ava Willett

*for Lisel Mueller*

ALSO BY LINDA NEMEC FOSTER:

# Contents

# III.

# A Note from the Author

For any poet and writer, to complete a manuscript of new work is a cause for celebration. To get that manuscript accepted by an amazing press (given the highly competitive nature of the publishing industry) only accentuates the great celebratory vibe. That was my experience when Nancy Eimers, the editor of New Issues Press, accepted my full-length collection of poems, *The Blue Divide*, for publication in 2019. The book was published in the spring of 2021, nominated for a number of book awards, and received a glowing review in *Publishers Weekly*. I was so grateful to Nancy and her staff at Western Michigan University for bringing *The Blue Divide* into the world.

That being said, you can imagine my sadness when New Issues closed its doors due to challenging economic circumstances in June 2023. *Huffington Post* described the press as having "the best qualities of the publishing tradition." Words of praise indeed. And with those words, you can also imagine my celebratory vibe when another fine and amazing university press offered to assume the editorial responsibilities of keeping *The Blue Divide* in print and in distribution worldwide. Cornerstone Press, sponsored by the University of Wisconsin–Stevens Point, was that amazing press. I am very grateful to Dr. Ross K. Tangedal, Director and Publisher, for accepting *The Blue Divide* (for a second time) and keeping it alive in the world.

What you're now holding in your hands is the second edition—another reincarnation, if you will—of *The Blue Divide*. All the poems are here along with the fine blurbs from Jim Daniels, Robert Fanning, Cecilia Woloch, and Laurel Blossom—and that wonderful review from Publishers Weekly. I'm so pleased this book is still walking in the world and continuing "to map what flows between us" (to quote from Fanning's blurb). Again, my deep gratitude to Dr. Tangedal and the entire editorial team at Cornerstone Press. Long live poetry and its readers.

Linda Nemec Foster
Grand Rapids, Michigan
March, 2024

# I.

*Oh as I was young and easy in the mercy of his means,*
*Time held me green and dying*
*Though I sang in my chains like the sea.*

—Dylan Thomas, "Fern Hill"

# Love in the Midst of War

You attempt to name the image
that cannot be named. As if a stone
could become the cold heart
of a grenade, a clenched fist
of twisted metal. As if a simple
artery could become barbed wire,
a menacing circle of grappling hooks.

Choose public or private violence—
war or the aftermath of love and
distinguish one from the other.
The young man covered with dark tattoos
reading the wedding announcements
could be the armed guard greeting the foreign
tourist at every train station. Only
the silent moon surrounded by the gray
of shrapnel and transparent clouds
knows how to tell the difference.

# The Cypress Trees in Croatia

The women speak as if they are singing
and who can blame them; their war
ended only twenty years ago. The bullet holes
from the Serbian guns still visible
in the walls of the fire station in Dubrovnik.

But how do they sing? Their low Slavic
voices have long abandoned the illusion
of perfect pitch. They know it's a myth,
a fragment of a mermaid's song. Their mouths
would rather mimic the air around the cypress trees,

trees standing sentinel to hillsides that have
witnessed too much silence. Their mouths
embrace the cold, numbing air of *bura*, the wind
of November that echoes their voices as
they sing from the valley of their throats.

# Report from Bosnia: "Hair" Performed in Sarajevo

The Age of Aquarius
is sung in broken English
to a packed house
in a small room.
The actors do not
take off their clothes
at the play's finale
("we're already naked
from the war," one
singer says). But
they ask the audience
to sing and join them
on a tiny stage.

They perform only
when there's electricity:
more than a dozen
performances have been
interrupted or stopped
because of mortar shells.

The artistic director
who also doubles
as the bass guitarist
plays with a gun
strapped to his waist.
Black revolver stolen
from the cold grip
of a dead Serb.

A young boy sitting
on his mother's lap
in the fourth row

smiles for the camera.
"My name begins
with 'A'," he says
through an interpreter,
"just like Aquarius."

Next week he will
be killed with 8 others
standing in line for bread.
At his grave, there is only
his picture nailed
to a wooden board.
No name.
They've run out of letters.

# The American Insomniac Buys Lipstick in Warsaw, 1950

The tourist has no idea
what is fashionable here.
Her confused circadian clock
can't even determine day
from night, so forgive her
for wanting only two colors
on her lips. One to echo
the honey glow of sun,
the other to resonate
the blue aura of moon.

But how could she know
Stalin would (in effect)
abolish all color—
no Tangerine Blush /
Tropical Melon / Scarlet Freeze—
no Rouge Violet / Raspberry Glace /
Mauve Cooler. Only lipstick
by numbers. The digits randomly
assigned in some outdated
cosmetics factory on the outskirts
of town. Peach Melba becomes 855.
Rose Creme becomes 412 (matte) or
411 (semi-gloss). The numbers
slowly marching to infinity
on the shelf of an empty store.

As if this calibrated palette
could be authentic. Not Michelangelo
illuminating the creation
of Man, but a faceless socialist
painting Sobieski's palace frescoes
by number. Not *David* in Florence,

but the granite breasts of the massive
Soviet woman sculpted into a bureaucrat's
gray office building on Plac Konstytucji.

The bureaucrat whose days
are filled with dreams
of women in hot-pink
G-strings. Whose nights
are filled with staring
at the crowded and desolate
streets. Across the square,
the tourist paints her lips
too red. The color
overwhelming the face
that looks back at her
from the borrowed mirror.

# Poland

*—for Jeff, in memoriam*

Because the thin strip of the Hel Peninsula juts out
    into the Baltic Sea like your ancestor's dream;
because it was near Gdańsk where Hitler began
    his invasion of Poland starting the horrific war
    that turned this country into the last century's
    graveyard, crematorium, dumping ground
    of desolation;
because it was here that Stalin conducted his land
    grab, his politics of duplicity, his transformation
    of the blue sky crowning Kraków's Royal Castle
    to the gray clouds belching
    from Nowa Huta's factories;
because so many died here--your family, my family,
    the young Jew hiding in the closet
    under the kitchen floor;
because despite all of this--the war, the camps,
    the constant shifting of borders, the country survived
    to become Europe's phoenix
    rising from the ashes of my great aunt's sister
    from Poznań, your anonymous cousin
    from a town south of Warsaw;
because this place of your ancestors means literally
    PO-LAND, people of the land,
    people of this plain in central Europe
    bordered by the Baltic in the north,
    the Tatra Mountains in the south,
    Prussian aggression in the west,
    Russian arrogance in the east,
    all the past histories silenced in the pure rain;
cleansing a meadow of wildflowers near Zakopane—
    sweet grass, purple lupine,
    white asters growing from bones;

cleansing the ancient trees in the primeval forest
     of Białowieża—graceful pines, towering oaks,
     rustling birches and their torn skins;
cleansing the dunes on the Baltic coast—fog
     that tries to embrace the sifting earth, lovers
     that cover their naked bodies with sand,
     the silent amber washed ashore;
cleansing the Obra River and its clouds of birds—
     golden eagles, black woodpeckers,
     long shadows of pure white storks;
because all the lands of your ancestors have been cleansed
     in tears, in blood,
     in fire, in exile,
     in forgiveness, in love,
     in truth, in expectation
     to welcome you home.

# Fire and Ice

A crowded bar on the other side
of the world. A stranger leans
into her blue scarf and whispers,
"Blue is something of an ecstatic
accident created by fire and ice."
The flamenco dancer in front of them,
her intense torso lighting
the small stage with a fire
so real they could feel it on their skin.
Waves of red and gold—a sunset
flaming from her arms and arched
back. No ice blue dawn but dusk
of the lost hours between silence
and word. His open mouth.
The space between them evaporating
in the heat of what happened next.

## Café de Paris: Geneva, Switzerland

The restaurant only serves one entreé with two side orders—steak, salad, and french fries—that's it. It's that simple. No need for menus, no need to read French or Italian or German, no need to stutter with an American accent. The widower from Brussels at the next table had a wife who was a vegetarian. She wouldn't be caught dead in a place like this. The smell of the meat would be enough to put her over the edge. She's dead, so it's a moot point. But not for her husband who still dreams her alive. He remembers (like it was just last week) how she berated him for eating a greasy hamburger. Not because it was greasy, but because it came from a cow. Just like the quiet cows that dot the Swiss countryside outside Geneva. Just like the cow he's eating now: medium rare, slightly bloody. His wife hated meat but approved of the ancient world's ritual of gazing at slaughtered animals' entrails to predict the future. He envisions her frown appearing in the reflection of the red juices pooling on the plate. Her mouth opens in disbelief: *You moron! What do you think you're doing, eating in a place like this that doesn't even know what tofu is? Think of your heart. Your congested, breaking heart.*

# Pictures of the Floating World: New York City, June, 2001

We all want to be famous,
or at least, remembered,
so we endlessly document
our little lives. Take
photographs of every
gesture. A man in a rowboat
floats around the island
of Manhattan and declares
his journey as historically
viable as Ponce de León's.
In other words, his life
as a bona fide miracle.
And, like magic, the skyline
emerges from the East River:
a potent mix of reality TV
and mirage. What we see
are long shots of sky-
scrapers, close-ups
of the man, his friends,
his dog, the abandoned
warehouse by the river's
edge, the desolate field
at the base of a bridge.
What we can't imagine
is just outside the camera's
memory. The twin towers
gone. The landscape slashed.
The man in his boat becoming
as forgettable as an ordinary
day when they still existed.

## NYC to Poughkeepsie: The Man on the Train

How can I begin to tell you the frayed story
of my empty life? The endless days
of endless commutes on trains filled
with strangers. If "gray" had a face
you'd see my blank stare right next
to the word in the dictionary.
Grapple, grasp, grating, then me—
gray—my whole existence
stuffed into four letters. My body
stuffed into this bird suit. See my tired
plumage. See the wings that tried
to abandon the nest. The sound of air
as the hollow bone embraces it.

# The Dead

always leave things behind:
gaudy topaz ring of a mother,
silent harmonica of a father,
a favorite uncle's shot glass,
a forgotten aunt's bone china.
The list spirals into a litany of
convoluted loss, so it's really
no surprise when her husband
brings her "a surprise gift."
The stained fragment of a small
animal's spine that he found
near the maple tree. Eight perfect
vertebrae aligned like train cars
or a Lego toy her son lost
in the backyard. She remembers
a story overheard at a funeral
in Lansing. How a philosophy
professor stole a thigh bone
from an archeological dig
in Peru, something a young
Inca girl left behind just for him
to find. At least that's what
his ego whispers in his ear.
But what of the "almost dead,"
what do they leave? The three
girls locked in a house in Cleveland
by a bus driver. Ten years later
and they're women who finally
escape; they leave nothing.
Fill their bodies with nose studs,
eyebrow rings, stark red and green
tattoos of roses and thorns.
And that arrogant academic

who used the girl's femur for
a paperweight? He died, too.
The unpublished manuscript
of his life's work on Nietzsche
collecting dust in a cousin's attic.

# Inside the Crater

No iridescent gems to blind us. No tropical paradise either.
The inner landscape of Diamond Head—the inside of that iconic
crater—reminds me of a dried meadow, a yellow field in central
Kansas used for the county fair's overflow parking. Who
would've guessed this tourist magnet would be boring?
That the community college across the street with its stunning
cactus garden would be more intriguing to our midwestern eyes?
The view from the rim might be Kodak-moment gorgeous,
but we're talking about the crater here—and it's a dud.

And how many duds have we sustained in our collective
lifetimes? Ex-husbands and former lovers. Small towns
and dying cities. Our old neighborhoods in Detroit might
as well be the streets of Dresden, circa 1945: houses
bombed out, abandoned, torn down. Even the crazy
people are gone. No more bag lady screaming at strangers
on Cass Ave. and bathing in the sink of a public restroom.
No more belligerent neighbor slaughtering pigs with a dull
knife in his garage on Irvington. That place is in the past.

The past. Like your first apartment in Honolulu off Monsarrat.
So close to the zoo, you heard the screams of the caged
animals every night. But before their laments, you heard
the sounds of the common birds at dusk. Dull sparrow
and awkward peacock competing for your attention.
That's when you lived so close to Diamond Head
you told me in a late-night phone call you could almost
touch it like a forgotten postcard taped to the *lanai*.

You still live in the middle of that ocean, on that island
created by dying volcanoes. Diamond Head still in your
landscape and Detroit still in mine. I went back to Michigan
and stayed there. The difference so great, sometimes when
I call you from my side of the world, I'm already in tomorrow.

# Transplant

"Tropical plants don't have an imagination or sense of humor,"
says the man on Oahu. He can't understand why the *haole*
tourists think this is paradise. *This* meaning this island
anchored in the middle of the Pacific Ocean. Born in Boston,
he spent 40 years teaching in "paradise" (he put those quotes
around the word—not me). He hated the place so much,
on the weekends away from the harsh fluorescent lights
of the classroom and his bored, half-somnolent students,
he took pictures of Hawaii that the tourists would only ignore.

> The overflowing trash dumpsters
> by the cinderblock apartments on King Street.
> The homeless drunk passed out behind the statue
> of Duke Kahanamoku on Kūhiō Beach.
> Half-dead palm trees stunted by trade winds
> taking a wrong turn and getting lost on Wilder Ave.

This is the face of paradise never mentioned in the *AAA Guidebook
to the Hawaiian Islands* that occupies space on a retiree's bookshelf
in Brookline. But no image of any less-than-perfect sunset,
no rainbow too faint to notice, no cloudy and bland day
can explain his one recurring dream: his empty classroom
transported to the hills above Waimea Bay where hundreds
of floating hau flowers litter the valley's river. The crimson
blossoms oblivious to his shadow as he tries to count each one.

# Six Days: A Creation Myth

## I.

The markings of the world:
disc of desert blur,
concentric sphere imagining itself
divided and conquered.
A man's rusted compass,
a woman's hint of blue shadow.

## II.

The heart as a spiral.
Red path engraved with dates,
postmark of memory.

## III.

Math of desire:
addition of "I want"
subtraction of "you want"
caught in the web of signs.
Love's artifact filled with
whose heaven, whose earth?

## IV.

How music begins—
captured birdsong
blank lines
silence.

## V.

Connect the letters
to create the garden's apple
perfect red and its echo.

## VI.

Stars as necklace
bird as witness
glass as vapor
all embraced
from the beginning.

# Scar

The last time I saw her (the woman
who once was a close friend), I swear
her dead husband kept calling her cell phone.
It rang constantly. No voice on the other end.
Was it the new boyfriend from Florida
(like she thought) hanging up before
he got up the nerve to say her name?
Or was it just Bill trying to edge back
into her life from his ceramic urn deposited
somewhere in upstate New York?

The last time I saw her, she told me
to drive her used Chevy down a country
two-track overgrown with waist-high
field grass and mud. The reason: she thought
he lost something there back when he was still
alive and married. A key chain, a black glove.
Doesn't matter now; we got stuck.

Two men who appeared out of nowhere—
shirtless, with cigarettes and pagers
stuffed into their pockets—rocked us out.
Guardian angels or accidental footnotes,
their bodies eventually retreated
from the rearview mirror as I looked
straight ahead and shifted the gears.
She didn't say a word. Back at her house,
a heavy rain. The tired peonies had lost
all their blossoms. A deep coral littered
the driveway right up to the front door.

# Trying to Get It Right

> *"Very often knowing yourself isn't really going to lead you anywhere."*
>
> —Diane Arbus

That dream you dreamt last night isn't about you or me or being lost in a ghost town that resembles what Ypsilanti would look like if it was nuked. Nuked down to nothing but a convoluted labyrinth of underground tunnels, dark catacombs, sleepless nights. That dream is about you trying to get it right: the perfectly juxtaposed metaphor, flowing enjambment, a closing line to die for. But there are no simple lessons here, only the maze of caverns under burned-out Ypsilanti. Ourselves lying down together on the damp ground—eyes closed, fingers barely touching. We listen to some self-appointed poetry guru in a three-piece suit (as gray as his gray eyes) talk about How To Do It. From couplets to coupling, from exotic villanelle to rondeau of the familiar. He's as arrogant as an erection, as blank as a masked man at an outdated costume ball. In other words— all illusion. In other words—all lies. What you do next is up to you. Move an inch and redesign your Michigan basement. Sit up and watch your daughter play sex games with the boy next door. Awaken and begin writing the very first line of your very first poem. You'll be amazed at how easy it is. And how difficult. Like the impression made by your body on that cavern floor, left by a stranger.

# Sequence: The Artist's Notebook

## I. How to Paint an Approaching Storm

Pick a clear day while they still exist.
Blue sky, yellow sun, the predictable boredom
of a calm landscape. Blend in the anxiety
of waiting: the cicadas suddenly hushed;
the hawk lost in its endless spiral.
Keep mixing the afternoon in colors
that are silent: gray of stone, black of
the stone's shadow, the palette
of dusk arriving too soon. Close your eyes
and count—to one hundred, to your birthday,
to the square root of memory until the sky
splits into a crooked river of light. Now stop.
Feel the rain on your face as if for the first time.
As if you have never been here before.

## II. The American and His Wife Dream in Florence

Of course, they would dream in this city
full of art and the human yearning to create
the divine. In the husband's dream, he becomes
Fra Angelico—complete with Dominican robes
and a frescoed wall in a Florentine monastery.
He paints *The Annunciation*. Imagines Gabriel,
the rainbow-colored wings; the concave body of Mary,
waiting to be filled. Her hands crossed in such
tenderness, he cries himself awake and startles his wife
from her dream. She was swimming in the air, a small
girl floating in the gilded corner of a Baroque ceiling.
The walls covered with mirrors, the floor covered with pearls.
Silent, except for the sound of a boy counting each one.
His hands filled with small moons, his voice filled with her name.

## III. Portrait

More than twenty years before his Mona Lisa,
he painted me, Ginevra, a young woman from Florence
who married too young and died too soon. No wonder
I look beautiful and distracted. No hint of a smile
to tempt you with speculation. I'd rather dream
of the landscape behind me: dark clouds of juniper
echoing my name; soft rumor of trees reflecting
memory. Who will remember me? My arms and hands
are missing (unlike the famous Mona). I could blame
the artist but what's the use? It's not easy being *here*,
motionless, with my "beauty adorning virtue."
His words, not mine. The perfect caption for a bride
who has no chance to turn back and disappear.
Disappear into that invented landscape of sky and water.

## IV. Back Story

The open mouth of St. Teresa and her ecstasy.
The death of Blessed Ludovica and its mirage of light.
Pluto's wide hand on the marble thigh of Proserpina
and the tears that seem to stream down her cheek.
All of this passion by Bernini can overwhelm
any young tourist, but it's his Daphne and Apollo—
the girl growing leaves and roots while the god
is in hot pursuit—that makes my daughter gasp,
"better than Michelangelo." But she doesn't know
Bernini's back story: the jealous rage that made him force
a servant to slash a woman's face until it wasn't a face.
But why ruin the moment? No artist is perfect
even though the art can be. Consider his Teresa and
her angel. The marble floats as if it's already in heaven.

V. Art and Life

Who can sculpt grief like Michelangelo?
His writhing slaves, incomplete and still locked
in their marble wombs, mirrored an agony
only matched by his. He knew how to perfect it
on the silent face of a perfect Madonna. Mother
and dead son. But imagine this other grief:
at the moment when another woman's grown
son died—not by crucifixion but by cancer—she
crawled into his hospital bed, held him, and sang
lullabies until he was cold. What image embraces
the deeper pain? The art enshrined in a large church?
Or the private tableaux hidden in a corner of suburbia?
Our master of grief cannot answer. Only asks another
question from the silent marble growing from his hands.

VI. The Modern Artist Laments the Post, Post-Modern World

When will it end? This incessant march
towards deconstructing the already too-fragile
world. Performance artists shun old-fashioned
nudity in favor of wearing raw meat dresses and
skyscraper high heels that look like horse hooves.
Even Duchamp's descending nude can't compete
with the image of a cow's tendon covering
the pale breasts of a woman in Soho. Her hat—
a giant halo, a giant stuffed sting-ray—
flapping in the breeze. She'd rather eat it
(*I'll eat my hat!*) than attend any "outdated"
exhibit with (and I'm quoting here) *that flat
stuff on the walls, stuck in those boring frames.
The lonely islands of three dimensions, static in the air.*

## VII. Gift

A year before my son met the woman he'd marry,
you painted this landscape of rocks, water and thin line
of horizon. The place consumed by a lake and its obsession
with the idea of blue. The idea hugs the shore and won't
let go: not for the stark branch insisting on its existence;
or the boulders losing their sense of decorum with wild
layers of movement. Isn't that how love works?
The spinning and falling, obsessing and wondering what
happens next. The view from this high bluff can't predict
the future—let alone the future of our children,
"impossible to know from this height." All we can do
is give the gift and tell them to hold on—to each other,
to that idea of blue. The expanse of the landscape that can't
be contained in a single image. That's what you give them.

# The Dream of Maine

*—for Margo Carlson Berke*

You've never been there
but your hands imagine
this place where land,
sea, and sky come together
so effortlessly, it reminds you
of the perfectly woven cloth—
seamless, like water.

And, just as effortlessly, the brown
hill rises from the beach
and rocks become green-covered
with strands of kelp, like tossed
hair combed by the ocean. As if
every color you layer on the paper's
surface leaves your hand
and creates its own life—
as persistent as the clouds
overwhelming any hint of blue.

But what is beyond the horizon
of this place you've never seen?
Only this: you surrounded by Maine.
Not a mere longing in your heart,
but Maine. And your son
still young enough to hold
in your arms and the deep cobalt
of the ocean, a small gesture away.

## Milan, Ohio

It's pronounced My´-lan not Mi-lan´
(as in the iconic city in northern Italy).
Here in northern Ohio, people don't care
about icons unless you mention Edison,
the town's favorite son made famous
when he invented artificial light.
11:39 PM and the place can't be bothered
with history or trivial facts:
        what Tom ate for breakfast;
        the name of the family dog;
        the childhood disease that caused his deafness.
11:40 PM in late December and the snow
already tires of the season. Doesn't even
notice the shadow of a car passing
through to somewhere else. Passenger-side
caved in, right headlight missing, three
windows splintered into diamond fragments.
A woman is in that car navigating the back
roads of Edison's childhood, trying
to get to the nearest friendly light.
In the dark, she can discern the muted
contours of a small town cemetery. Her night
vision heightened by the fact that hours
earlier she survived a freak accident
on the turnpike: side-swiped by a truck,
sending her car spinning in convoluted circles,
the impact shattering the windows as if
the breath of God was trying to tell her
something. Tonight, the details of his
whisper don't matter. Only the fact
she's alive, driving the car off the highway,
finding the two-lane roads through Berlinville,

South Amherst, Gambier, Milan. Separating
the dark from the near dark, not as assured
as the inventor born here, not as absolute
as the Spirit hovering over the road, but
as a woman given another chance to see
and chart the map of her life's landscape.
The living and the dead.

# Fashion Accessories for the Seven Deadly Sins

### Sloth—Handbag

A slug, a snail, a handbag of flesh. Flesh-colored mascot of my only daughter. That lazy kid who won't make her bed, do her laundry, finish that goddamn term paper on time. What to do but keep quiet; let her sling that faux leather purse over her shoulder as she makes her slow exit out of my life.

### Lust—Black Stiletto Heels

Hot, black idols of desire. All orifice and no thought. Not even that tempting snake from the oh-too-perfect garden can come up with any excuse for it. Lust as the one sure thing to keep us up at night, the double helix unraveling: yes/no. The wanton snake split in two, the shoes we hide under our beds.

### Anger—Red Lipstick

Bullet with your name on it. Red streak of the drive-by shooting: small caliber gun with the safety off, the hammer cocked, fragments of bullets, exit wounds. You're pissed as hell and want the whole world to know it. The slick blood yelling your name to everyone in the universe, to no one in particular.

### Pride—Mirror

I'm the king of the hill, the top banana, the belle of the ball. Look at me and see—me. Every little piece of me, broken and ricocheted into the black hole that doubles as an eye. One long look at past/present/future, but especially forever. The image of myself that keeps repeating the cold, hollow echo.

Greed—Cell Phone With Rhinestones

I want, I want, I want everything/everyone/all the time. I want to collect the world in my ear. All of it—from every string of gossip hanging from an acquaintance's lips to beaded fabrications of world events. Macrame of wars and rumors of wars. Speed dial your life into mine, let it fall into my open, empty ear.

Envy—Tinted Contact Lenses

I'm not one-eyed or green-eyed. I'm like Argus, Juno's slacker, whose vast array of eyes landed in the peacock's tail. I see it all. I see what you have and want it—no questions asked. I
certainly don't want to bother you with fake tears. Just hand it over, make it simple, do it now.

Gluttony—Navel Stud

The bigger, the better. The undulating stomach protrudes and is good. Let's show some midriff, let's show some skin, let's eat and drink. And to mark the center of our digestive tract (the center of our universe) let's place a perfect chip of rose quartz. Like a tiny remnant of a pink tongue willing to swallow anything.

# II.

*...if only you could see*
*how heaven pulls earth into its arms*
*and how infinitely the heart expands*
*to claim this world, blue vapor without end.*

—Lisel Mueller, "Monet Refuses the Operation"

# Fog Made of Iron

*"The universe really is a weird place."*

—Allan Boss

*OK, listen to this.*
*Astronomers just discovered*
*a planet that is so airy*
*it has the density*
*of Styrofoam. And*
*somewhere else*
*there's a planet*
*where the surface*
*temperature reaches*
*3100 degrees,*
*where the gray fog*
*is so dense*
*it's made of iron.*
*Imagine the irony*
*of iron raindrops,*
my daughter
nonchalantly posits
as she stirs her coffee.

I respond with a simple
nod. Yes, I can
imagine this universe
of irony where daughters
turn from students to teachers,
where mothers turn
from lectures to silence,
where even the sun
turns on its axis without
holding on. And the sky
must release every

cloud to become blue,
blue, pure blue
before the dark night
can release any star.
Those small lights
that outline Cassiopeia
and her Andromeda.

# Anonymous Afternoon

*"I have invented a new genre, that of silence."*
—Isaac Babel

The man in the red shirt is in love with the green carpet.
Its speckled edges of gray, the orange slash of color
in the far corner of the room. Its silence. If it could talk,
the man knows the carpet would sound as confident
as a fortune cookie:

*Happy news is on its way.*
*Tomorrow will be a productive day,*
          *don't oversleep.*
*Remember three months from this date!*
*Your lucky star is shining.*

Shining, shining like this afternoon where there is nothing
to do except watch the carpet be nothing but a carpet.
There's always the window and its cavalcade of blue sky
or that huge oak tree pointing its huge fingers
at a random cloud. But the silence of the carpet is better.
Somewhere there is someone who is just about to

## The Far Country

A week after your death, I dreamed
I was on a train in a foreign country.
No passport, no money, nothing but my name.
An old woman who claimed to be the great,
great-granddaughter of the great Leo Tolstoy
was sitting beside me in the aisle seat,
wearing an elaborate wedding gown. Not white
but off-white. Ivory, a color my mother
used to call "candlelight," a color reserved
for non-virgins. The woman clutched a copy
of *The Norton Anthology of World Masterpieces*
as if it were a Bible. The huge tome filled
with the dust of dead writers. I turned
to look at the book and that's when I saw you:
sitting across from me, pressed against the window
of the train as if there was no tomorrow.
And I had to tell you that no, you didn't
have any tomorrows waiting to greet you
like the blurring green landscape flashing by
our muted eyes. "My friend, you're dead."
You looked amused—then stunned and shocked—
as you began to speak a litany of words
only the Tolstoy relative could understand;
a combination of Slavic syllables that sounded
like rain seeping into the earth. I knew
you had already begun a different journey.
And I left you on that train still transfixed
at the window. I had to leave you there,
my friend, and walk alone to the borderlands,
to the place that separates us. The far country
where the border lies hidden and the guards
look distracted, asking for nothing but your name.

## Mount Fuji

My friend always wanted to see the mountain
with its eternal snow, but she never
crossed the ocean to Japan. Instead,
she bought a small reproduction
of Hokusai's "Boy Viewing Mount Fuji"
and hung it on her bedroom wall.
Every morning it greets the daylight:
the boy with his back to her
as he faces the mountain and plays a flute,
his body perfectly balanced on a thick
tree branch that seems to slice
Fuji's heart with a rugged abandon.
"In another life," she vows, "I'll come back
as that flute, the hollow reed content
to be held and hidden in the boy's hands."

## All That We Cannot Name

Your eye sees one thing,
the camera imagines another.
Shape disappears into weightless blue,
light becomes a shadow's mirror.
Image floats to the surface
like a language you've never heard:
fluid lines of exotic characters.
As if an ancient riddle poses a question
in the momentary stillness
of the camera's held breath
and you know it will take
your whole life to learn the answer.

# The Atheist

She needs nothing, no one to affirm her existence. No crotchety Old Man in the Sky; no God Delusion (to paraphrase the title of one of her favorite books). She always keeps it on her nightstand, along with her other favorites: various international cookbooks; how to paint cheap furniture to look expensive; how to bake elaborate cakes that can be mistaken for soft sculpture or misplaced genitalia. She's an atheist because she believes in only one body—hers. Not even her husband's is interesting now. With its balding head and flabby skin. A caricature of his former self. Unlike her own body that worships at the plastic surgeon's altar: uplifted eyelids, liposuctioned hips and thighs, erased creases where worry once lived. She scoffs at the church wedding but desperately wants to be invited to the reception so she can scope out the wedding cake. Does it live up to all the retouched photographs in *Wedding Cakes and You: The Perfect Marriage*? Her ultimate favorite book. She says it reads like a memoir without the pathetic whining. She dreams of baking the perfect wedding cake for a son, a daughter—enough cake and frosting to feed hundreds; no, thousands. A better trick than that uneducated carpenter from the north country. How dare he change water into wine and consider it a miracle. How dare you believe it. You with your constant hunger, open mouth, empty hands.

# Waiting for the Annunciation

*(after the painting "Waiting" by Nancy Wanka)*
*"Art does not imitate life. Art anticipates life."*
—Jeanette Winterson

No sacrilege here, only art. And not
the kitschy art of the Madonna of the Suburbs,
nestled in a bathtub grotto near the garage—
the limp shirts on the line, her only devotees—
but real art: a young girl in an empty room.
I could see the screaming headline now,
*Free-Spirit Agnostic Chosen to be God's Mother,*
and the ensuing media frenzy. The reporters
just concentrate on her face and don't notice
the immense yellow space at her right. Too
brilliant; as if the sun had forgotten its place
in the sky and wanted to sit down beside her.
What is she thinking with her doubting eyes
averted? The sideways glance too busy sizing up
the colors of citron and corona, sunflower and pollen
to really notice the face of God just outside
her sphere of reference: the pale gray hood,
the deep blue jacket. These colors of the sky
groom her to be another version of a modern
madonna waiting for someone to call her name. But
no angel wings announce *Mystery Happening Right Now.*
And as for any boyfriend waiting on the sidelines...
Forget it. Whether his name is Joe or Mike or
Kevin, she'll break a heart and total the car.
Smashed fender the least of his worries. But
back to her waiting to say *yes* or *no.* At the moment,
she's alone. Apart from everyone. Even thoughts
of mother/father, daughter/son. Any second now,
the whole world will stop holding its breath.

# The Modern Woman Imagines
# the Life of Mary Magdalene

## I. Washing Christ's Feet with Her Tears

Her mother must have just died.
That's why the guilt and crying
and feeling oh-so-sorry.
So sorry, she starts making up sins
to confess: cursing the cat, refusing
to cook dinner, forgetting to make
the bed. Simple domestic sins
that God disguised as a man
could identify. Her trumped-up charges
loosen her hair, sting his feet.

## II. The Rising of Lazarus

She never really knew him,
although rumor had it
he was her brother.
Long-lost, long-gone, long-forgotten.
Hard to remember him or a time
of normalcy: mother/father, sister/brother.
But here he is—smack in the middle of her life—
because some part of her wanted him alive
again, wanted him to rise from the dead.
It wasn't exactly Magdalene who asked
the favor; she only witnessed the aftermath.
Wondering how long this second life would last,
imagining the strange permanence of his second death.

## III. "Don't You Touch Me," He Said

After all of it is done:
the long night of sweating in a garden;

a friend's kiss of betrayal;
another friend's losing a bet
with a servant and a rooster;
the beating and spitting;
the bleeding and falling;
the nailing up and tearing down.
After all of it is done—
that is, after he's finally dead—
he still won't leave her alone.
Days later and she sees him,
a solitary figure pruning an olive tree.
Could be a mirage or a gardener,
a former lover or distant stranger.
Doesn't matter. She still can't touch
him. Her hand lost in what appears
to be only a shadow, the breeze at dusk.

IV. Preaching to the Rich

Here's a first: the only woman
dressed in rags    (correct that—

               dressed in hair—see Donatello's
               ravaged-in-wood Magdalene in Janson's
               *History of Art*)
to berate and belittle the rich.
She doesn't even preach on their level,
but above them, in a pulpit carved
from a thick cypress. What to make
of this history-making event? No TV camera
or news photo could contain it
in a simple caption, a stilted video screen. You'd need
the sound and fury of pure digital streaming.
The Magdalene encased in red hair
breathing fire and brimstone, the stark food
she inhales for breakfast, lunch, and dinner.

## V. The Magdalene Leaves for France

She's tired of the crowds and their social network.
All done with trying to win the popularity contest.
Buys a rudderless boat and sets sail for
Anywhere But Here,
leaves Palestine and its gossip and dust behind.
She lands in Marseilles and picks a cave
in the wilderness to call home. The mountains
around the grotto embrace her like an open fist:
the true enigma (Bride of Christ, Fiancée of John the Baptist),
the pure invention that she is.

## VI. The Angel Brings Food to Her Cave

Describe the angel, Magdalene, not the menu.
Archangel or just plain angel, throne
or principality, dominion or power, seraphim
or cherubim. Or was it simply your guardian
angel doing what comes naturally—surrounding
you with wings until the hunger
left your body. And can you describe
those wings? Multi-colored rainbow
of Fra Angelico's *Annunciation* or marble gray
of Bernini's *Ecstasy*? Choose one or the other.
The wings expanding your life from whore to saint.

## VII. She Receives Her First Communion

She didn't have time to go out
and buy the perfect communion dress:
white taffeta underskirt, rolls of chiffon
and organza, a hint of satin ribbon
for a sash. And who could think
about pearls at a time like this...
in the middle of a cave in the south of France?
Let's assume she lacked fashion sense,

let's assume she refused to cut her hair
after it touched his feet. Her hair, down
to her ankles, becomes the perfect veil. She greets
the host covered with nothing but herself.

## VIII. Death of the Magdalene

At the exact moment of death,
your body that had been covered
for decades with the penitent's
hair, rags, and animal skins—
rabbit fur, dog hair, yellow tufts
of something else's life—your body
became pure gold. If the pungent
odor of myrrh had a face,
it would be yours. The visage
emblazoned with the dream of death.
Yours and his. The Christ and his lover.
Your lips, your lips on his feet.

## IX. She Ascends into Heaven

She didn't know what to expect.
The long spiraling journey upward
her auburn hair caught in the clouds
her breasts losing all sense of sensuality
the angels lifting her body, their wings,
the intense light, her mind shrugging off
memory as if it was last night's dream—
her perplexed, perplexing soul finally alone
with the one true object of her desire.

# Life Cycle of Clouds

## I. Sky

Layers of clouds that hint
of bird feathers, their flight lost
in an unending spiral of change.
What is not here, what is transformed.
Cumulus begets a young girl,
the bracelet uneven around her wrist.
Cirrus begets filaments of pearl.

## II. Earth

The shot heard round the world.
Not Sarajevo in 1914 or Gdańsk in 1939
or Dallas in 1963. Not textbook history but
personal myth. A kitchen window shattered in Detroit.
The man and his wife frozen on the next page.

## III. Sea

The last dream begins with a blue sky
to reclaim what has been lost. The wound
disappearing into a faint scar of cloud birth. Face
becoming blossom becoming starburst becoming sea.

# III.

*I woke up. I opened my eyes.*
*I touched the world as if it were a carved frame.*
—Wisława Szymborska, "Memory at Last"

# The Immigrants in Slavic Village: Cleveland, 1955

The Hungarian kids wear thin jackets missing
buttons. Stain of paprika in their mouths.
The Czechs pretend they know everybody's secrets
even those of Slovak Joe who spits at their shadows.
The Ukrainians can't stand the only neighbors
who can understand their language: those goddamn
Russians who starved their grandparents to death
in the twenties. The Lithuanians refuse to open
the blinds after dusk; something about the night
air stealing the breath of infants. And the Poles,
those men and women in love with the Black
Madonna, wash their hands before touching
their children—the sons and daughters as pale as water.
At night, the moon gets tangled in the open arms
of the dead oak tree on Salem Avenue and
can't decide if it's winter or spring, summer or fall.
The same bareness waits to embrace it every night.

# Family Tree

There was the rain in the mountains
of southern Poland. Nowy Sącz, the small
town caught in history's time warp: late
1800's and are we in Prussia or Austria?
What country defines this culture
of peasants? My great-grandfather,
the only blacksmith in a village
where horses outnumber people.

There was the dense forest
of intense birdsong. My grandfather
straining to understand the language
of dusk. Sparrows, with their dull
gray coats, complaining about the
Old World and its tight shoes.
"Get out, get out," they sing
in unison to the man who gambles
on a one-way ticket to Ellis Island.
Bribes the girl in the next village
to meet him in two years—
underneath the orange sky
above the steel mills of Cleveland.
Say "Cuyahoga," he tells her;
as if it were a river that ran
through her heart.

There was the exotic smell
of india ink on my father's
fingers when he came home
from work. Assembling printing
presses as big as garages, he
forgot the sound of words as
they left the page. He was only

interested in the machine's end
result: capturing letters
on an inked roller's surface.
By the time he died, he'd lost
the language of village and rain.

There was the echo of "I am"—
the confused ego of the immigrant's
granddaughter as she navigates
the New World. She has never
known the language of the Old
and she wants to be nothing
but American. Ageless, classless,
careless. She negotiates a history:
The Compromise of Opposites.
How to immigrate from one world
to another without realizing it.
She leaves her impression, her
empty outline on every major
street in America. Home of the
brave. Last image of an anthem.

There was the unrehearsed
arrival of the son: urban and
urbane. No hint of the rain
in the mountains, the fog
forgetting itself. He knows
only one language and uses
it to reinvent the past. No
history—only now. College
and small rooms. He'll visit
the mountains of Nowy Sącz
once and then instantly
misplace them. A postcard
in the very bottom drawer.

# Drawing: In the Evening, 1991

*(after Magdalena Abakanowicz)*

### I.

Old woman, who are you...
with your silent history
as deafening as a war?
The shadows surrounding each side
of your face could be hands
holding a gesture of surrender:
the white flag of cheekbone,
eye socket, straight nose,
closed mouth. Does the geometry
of dusk have a patron saint?
Is it you, solitary witness,
anonymous equation, collector
of the thin sound of night
as it envelopes the day?

### II.

You know who I am,
your grandmother forgotten
in the myth of your childhood.
The gray face of memory,
nostalgia. The fact that you
are the same age now
as I was when you were born—
impossible for you to accept
like a black cloud of starlings
overwhelming the sky. Look
at me watching you. Daughter
of my son, I will wash your regret
with my absent hands. Wrap you
tight in the blue damask of morning.

# The Theory of Everything

*"...a vision of physical reality so at odds with our experience
that it defies language."*

—The Teaching Co.

Einstein's theory of relativity can
be stated in one concise sentence.
But what is it? What noun
placed next to what verb
modified by what adverb
holds the secret? I ask my daughter,
the aspiring astrophysicist,
to speak the sentence; and if not
the concise sentence, then the undulating
lines of pure thought that describe
the theory of everything.
Her mother, who froze in high school
geometry, cannot comprehend how
tiny strings vibrating in
a microscopic universe can hold
everything together: from DNA's
double helix to the silky
translucence of a moth's wings
to Bach's Concerto for Two Violins.
How it can all be reflected
in eleven dimensions: eleven
parallel universes wrapped
in empty space—a dark energy
of nothing. My one-dimensional
mind boggles as my daughter explains.
But the messy world of an atom's nucleus
(the photons and quarks, the positrons
and muons, the wimps and Higg's Boson)
all blur in my tired head.

She describes a famous physicist's
lecture and I can only imagine
him at the podium with mismatched
socks. Dark blue of sky mistaken
for dark black of night. No use
searching my finite space for a unified
theory when I can hardly recognize
my own daughter as she lives
more and more in her own universe
and leaves my small world behind.

The daughter who waxes and wanes
like the moon; loves me
and pulls away like the tides;
listens to a rock group
called The Magnetic Fields sing
about the unscientific mess
of love; loses car keys
and forgets to turn off
the stove when the primordial
soup boils down to nothing.
The daughter who as a child
was lost in a Chicago museum
filled with the physics of Magritte;
and as a smaller child noticed
the silica shimmering
in a lake in Nova Scotia
and deemed it diamonds. This
woman who now peers at the stars
in the night sky and sees
the same brilliance. And
in the morning thinks the warm
air of a January thaw is not
fog, but the broken snow
on fire. The woman who knows

the textbook explanation, yet
wants to believe in the flames.

The daughter who looks at me
with my cosmology of tentative
words, tentative silence and tries
to see the mother: the proof
that experience does defy
all language. And everything,
everything is connected. Whether
we can dare to believe it or not.

# Blue

It must have been her accent
that seduced and baffled my ears.
The Egyptian woman, still lost
in the desert air of Cairo,
read her poems filled with water
from the Nile and blue heaven,
blue heaven, blue heaven flying
over the lotus flowers. I heard
"heaven" but later discovered
she said "heron." A distant cousin
to the sacred ibis, herons (even blue ones)
are commonplace—are everywhere—even
in the non-exotic marshes of northern Ohio
where another blue creation—my mother—
landed. Blue Helen, blue Helen, blue Helen.
The kids in Cleveland would tease her.
Her blue eyes swimming in the immigrant's
version of hide and seek, lost and found,
a lexicon of strange words that trip her tongue:

*thunder*

                                    *train track*

              *wind storm*

                                       *paradise.*

A paradise where she flies, dusts clouds,
and polishes haloes. Washing the blue
of heaven until it shines like a word
that has yet to be invented.

## The Water

My mother hated it, my father loved it.
The ocean between them so vast
not even two daughters could bridge
the blue divide. For him, it was natural
to choose Navy (not Army) when everyone
went to war after Pearl Harbor exploded.
He hopped on a supply ship, learned how
to navigate using nothing but the night sky.
Made his way to Normandy, Anzio, north Africa—
and back again—all in one piece. Brought
home a thin blanket and his uniform
both filled with the smell of sweat. His wife
couldn't wash it out; reminded of his ocean every day.

## Gravity and God

On her 90th birthday, my mother dreams
of her dead husband. "That would be
your father," she explains as if I wasn't
paying attention. After 60 years of marriage,
you can't blame her for forgetting he's gone:
the departure only six weeks ago.
She insists it really wasn't a dream
but his actual body materializing before her
and talking like "he always does"
gesturing with his hands about
what a pain-in-the-ass it is
to be where he is. He can't do anything anymore.
Drive his Buick, play golf, see Blaze Starr
at Roxy's Burlesque Theater on E. 9th Street.
My mother ignores his rants
like she always did. Except when he
starts talking about gravity and God—
not metaphysical theories of substance and spirit—
but the title of a song he wrote. Gravity and God:
A Song Without Words. He tells her only
the dead can sing it since they're not distracted
by brown grass or breathing. As he begins
to sing, the dream ends. Or as my mother
firmly states: "He leaves the room.
He was wearing that red sweater vest
and those baggy, gray slacks I hate."

# A Kiss Is Just a Kiss

*"It's the kissiest business*
*in the world. You have to keep kissing people."*

—Ava Gardner

My mother (in her own words)
                    "didn't know much,"
but what she knew, she knew.
How to darn a sock's hole until its universe
imploded into a white dwarf of string theories.
How to polish Window Wax into a mirror
until it reflected a gaze more intense
than Snow White's stepmother.
How to magically stir the cauldron of laundry
to transform Prussian bluing into a pure white shirt.

And then, her encyclopedic knowledge of movie stars.
She never called them actors or actresses but Stars.
As in the heavens, the constellations, the Big Bang.
Her lessons were taught by chain-smoking
gossip columnists. She poured over their theses
illuminated in the pages of *Confidential, The Lowdown,*
*Hush-Hush,* and *Uncensored.*

My mother could tell you:
how Jean Harlow really died
          "It wasn't kidney failure but she was poisoned
          by all that peroxide she used on her hair,"
how Greta Garbo brushed her teeth
          "She never used toothpaste—only salt,"
how Joan Crawford plucked her eyebrows
          "She didn't—enough said."

My mother loved the back-stabbing of it,
the kiss and tell of it, the guilty pleasure of it.

And when she read this quote from Ingrid Bergman—
  "A kiss is a lovely trick designed by nature
  to stop speech when words become superfluous"—
my mother (with her blue hands and absent husband) almost
believed it.

# At 68, My Mother Sees Her First Foreign Film

"What next?" my father laments,
as she gushes about *Jean de Florette*
as if she were a critic at Cannes.
How she admired the diligent hunchback
who loved flowers and tried to grow them
in the small plot he inherited in Provence.
How she hated the old local farmer
and his scheming nephew ("those creeps")
whose mindless greed for the hunchback's land
helped them devise a cruel plot.
How she marveled at the cruelty
of the plot to block and conceal
the natural spring that flows
into the hunchback's land and then
to pray for a drought. How she was aghast
that God answered the creeps' prayers.
How she pitied the poor hunchback
as he was forced to haul water
from a distant well, night and day,
day and night to save his precious
irises and jonquils, lilies and baby's breath.
How she wept when he died—
for him, for his wife, for his little girl
("who looked just like my Ellen"). All this emotion
from my mother pouring onto the kitchen
table. "What next?" my father moans.

He's afraid this is just the beginning.
Next week, she'll give up cold cuts
and blood sausage; start eating bean sprouts
and tofu. She'll begin to lose weight, get
svelte, buy stone-washed denim and gauze dresses.

She'll pierce her ears and then get bored
with Cleveland. She'll want to travel to someplace
exotic like....Fresno. Or, worse yet, she'll
get bored with him. Drop him for some weirdo
in a black beret who likes to sit in the dark,
listen to dialogue he can't understand,
and read subtitles. "What next?" my father sighs
as he contemplates his yellowing gallstones
and the muffled sound they make.

# Thirst

After the war, my father made
The Sign of the Cross—in the name
of the Father, and of the Son, and of the Holy Ghost—
whenever he entered the water.
A neighbor's swimming pool,
the murky waves of Lake Erie,
even tepid bath water
would evoke the same automatic response.
As if the shores of Normandy and Anzio,
Pearl Harbor and Guadalcanal
were more tangible, more real
than the quiet maple trees
outside his suburban front door.
Every night, he paced the basement:
a lost sailor trying to imagine the night sky
over Sicily. The Big Dipper pouring
its water to quench his thirst.

# In the Midst of Dreams

*(after the work of Jaume Plensa)*

## I. Disease

The father trapped in his body.
Disease of his mind closing
the door of his prison so tight
not even the idea of moonlight,
faint light of his dreaming self,
can escape. He shuts his eyes,
he memorizes the language
of regret, and it brands his face
like the lexicon of a sleepwalker.
"I should have planted the azaleas
in the month of rain.
I shouldn't have prayed so loud
to the silent face of God."
Endless words that fill
a small room with empty air.
He imagines his feet and the places
they have walked in the world:
the gray shores of Normandy
to the broken ridges of Montana.
After all these landscapes,
what shoes to wear at his funeral?
The possibilities surround him
like discarded souvenirs
from a forgotten vacation.
What can he do with the rest
of his life but pretend
he's a cloud? Dusk-tinged stratus
that marks his borderland,
the abandoned horizon.

## II. Hunger

The Spanish mystic cannot satisfy
his hunger. Locked in a cell
in Toledo, he envisions God
as a sharp wind,
a burning ember,
a vast mountain
only the night can embrace.
His hunger does not crave
any simple gesture,
bread and water once a day,
but only the bread of angels,
God Himself. How would the Divine
taste on his tongue? The mystic
closes his eyes and tries
to imagine swallowing pure light.
The radiance illuminating a path
from his mouth
to his heart
to his feet.
Who needs shoes for such a journey?
He remembers the ancient prophet
removing his unholy sandals
to approach the holy fire.
Fire that burned
but did not consume
until it flamed that night
in Toledo, in the belly
of the saint as he rehearsed
the language of heaven.

## III. Insomnia

The man who cannot sleep
has been here before: a room
filled with memory and the faint
sound of leaves as they cover
the ground. In the waking world,
he is an intruder, an interloper,
as uneasy in his skin
as the museum curator at Birkenau
discussing the glass cases
of shoes and hair. At night,
he is reduced to reinventing
every scenario of his life
from the opening credits
to the quiet denouement. His eyes
may not be open, but he remains
forever awake and counting.
Letters not syllables.
Words not ideas.
Phrases not sentences.
The people he has abandoned
scatter. But not before
they each leave their imprint:
fashionable leather boot,
small sneaker, red and
spiked heel, brown and
scuffed loafer. Each one demands
attention. Each one, a different
story he narrates in seamless
detail to the patient and faceless moon.

# The Muted Breath of Early Spring

This air looks like the muted breath
of early spring when the languishing
clouds, surrounded by the season's amnesia,
don't believe that winter's really gone.

This air sounds like the stifled cough
of harsh wind off Lake Erie. The forest
of my childhood where March startled
the maples into growing their leaves.

This air reminds me of why my father
cursed the irony of spring. Tentative
green of March covered
in an April ice storm.

And why he refused to die in the season
of "fake promises." He waited until July
to give summer his last breath.
And he did.

# On the First Anniversary of His Death, I Dream of My Father

I don't exactly dream of him, but his voice.
I'm calling from Kraków on the last night
of my trip. *Dad*, I speak into the white
phone. His voice on the other end sounds
deep and hoarse—as if he has a bad cold
or has been talking a lot. "Yeah," he replies.
*I'm in Kraków, your mother's city.*
"Oh, really, how's the weather?"
*Fine, it's been good.*

I want to tell him about this place
he's never seen. The Market Square
gleaming like afternoon light no matter
what time of day it is. The starlings
swooping like a black cloud in Grodzka Street
above the statues of the twelve Apostles.
Hearing my favorite Chopin nocturne
played in the Bonerowski Palace
by a young Japanese woman. ("Gee whiz,"
I could hear him say, "a Japanese woman
living in Kraków!"). How that nocturne
reminded me of him. The long
good-bye I never got to say.

But I just talk about inconsequential stuff:
the heat wave that turned into a soft rain
last night; the ugly Forum Hotel finally
boarded up and turned into a giant
billboard for Polish beer—the one and only,
Żywiec. "That's nice," he says.
"Well, I gotta go. I've been talking too much
over here and I don't want to lose my voice."

Somewhere on the edge of the city, a strong
wind embraces the birch trees, changing
their green leaves to silver in the thin morning.

## The Dream That Is Forgotten

like your mother's first language,
the thick, guttural sounds of Polish.
Forgotten because your mouth never
learned how to pronounce the letter
"Z" with three different accents. Forgotten
because you moved away from your grandparents,
those fearless immigrants who bartered Poland's
Tatra Mountains for the orange air of the Cleveland
steel mills. Forgotten because you wanted to forget
the past: embarrassment of long names
impossible to pronounce; the paper-thin hands
of the next-door neighbor and her pale face
getting lost in the backyard. Forgotten because you
wanted to escape Union Avenue, its cheap beer,
strong whiskey, and the radio static from the 2nd floor.

In the dream that is forgotten, you learn
to speak the language of sounds, not words.
Language of bark, leaves, stones, mud;
of fog sleeping in the marshes and sun caught
in tangled branches. Language of amber
sinking into its inclusions and rain falling
from its clouds. You try to remember each sound
as it leaves your lips, before you open your eyes
to the blank page.

ACKNOWLEDGMENTS

Grateful acknowledgment is made to the editors of the following magazines and journals, in which the following poems first appeared, some in slightly altered versions.

*1-70 Review*: "The Cypress Trees in Croatia," "Pictures of the Floating World: New York City, June, 2001," "Gravity and God"

*Apalachee Review*: "A Kiss Is Just a Kiss"

*basalt*: "Scar"

*Big Scream*: "Poland"

*Bloodroot Literary Magazine*: "Transplant"

*The Cresset Magazine*: "Anonymous Afternoon"

*Dominion Review*: "Trying to Get It Right"

*Driftwood Review*: "Fire and Ice," "The Water," "The Muted Breath of Early Spring"

*Earth's Daughters*: "Café de Paris: Geneva, Switzerland"

*The Fox Chase Review*: "The Dream of Maine"

*The MacGuffin*: "The Atheist," "Waiting for the Annunciation," "Drawing: In the Evening, 1991," "On the First Anniversary of His Death, I Dream of My Father," "The Dream That Is Forgotten"

*New Millennium Writings*: "Report from Bosnia: 'Hair' Performed in Sarajevo," "Fog Made of Iron," "Sequence: The Artist's Notebook"

*North American Review*: "Fashion Accessories for the Seven Deadly Sins"

*Passages North*: "NYC to Poughkeepsie: The Man on the Train," "Inside the Crater," "Thirst"

*Paterson Literary Review*: "The Immigrants in Slavic Village: Cleveland, 1955"

*Poetry Repair*: "All That We Cannot Name"

*Presa*: "Love in the Midst of War," "The Far Country"

*Presence*: "Milan, Ohio"

*Puerto del Sol*: "At 68, My Mother Sees Her First Foreign Film"

*Scintilla*: "Six Days: A Creation Myth"

*South Florida Poetry Journal*: "In the Midst of Dreams"

*Streetlight Magazine*: "The Dead," "Mount Fuji," "Blue"

*Two Review*: "The American Insomniac Buys Lipstick in Warsaw, 1950"

"Family Tree" was published in the anthology *The Heart of All That Is: Reflections on Home* edited by Jim Perlman, Deborah Cooper, Mara Hart, and Pamela Mittlefehldt (Holy Cow! Press, 2013).

"The Theory of Everything" was published in the anthology *Riffing on Strings: Creative Writing Inspired by String Theory* edited by Sean Miller and Shveta Verma (Scriblerus Press, 2008).

"Sequence: The Artist's Notebook" was the first runner-up in New Letters' Poetry Award, 2013 and it was a finalist in New Millennium Writings' National Competition, 2017.

"The Cypress Trees in Croatia" was nominated for a Pushcart Prize by the editors of *I-70 Review*, 2014.

"Blue" was nominated for a Pushcart Prize by the editors of *Streetlight Magazine*, 2017.

"In the Midst of Dreams" was commissioned by Frederik Meijer Gardens and Sculpture Park and was included in the exhibit brochure, *Poetry & Sculpture: Poetry based on the works of sculptor Jaume Plensa*.

\* \* \*

I would like to thank all my mentors and friends who have supported my work throughout my career: Lisel Mueller, Ellen Bryant Voigt, Stephen Dobyns, Heather McHugh, Faye Kicknosway, Colette Inez, Maria Mazziotti Gillan, Therese Becker, Miriam Pederson, Jack Ridl, Rodney Torreson, M.L. Liebler, Diane DeCillis, Dawn McDuffie, Kathleen McGookey, Pam Luebke, Leonard Kniffel, Richard Jansma, Herbert Woodward Martin, Ewa Parma, and John Guzlowski.

Special thanks to my family: Brian, Stephanie, and Lyla Foster; Ellen Foster; Deborah Nemec, Joe Cirincione; and Pete Foster.

Deep gratitude to the extraordinary editorial staff at New Issues Press: Nancy Eimers, Bill Olsen, and Kim Kolbe.

And, to my husband Tony—let me count the ways—your love is in every word, on every page.

LINDA NEMEC FOSTER has published thirteen collections of poetry, including *Bone Country* (Cornerstone Press), *Amber Necklace from Gdańsk*, *The Lake Michigan Mermaid* (2019 Michigan Notable Book), which was created with co-author Anne-Marie Oomen and artist Meridith Ridl, and *Talking Diamonds*. Her work appears in magazines and journals such as *The Georgia Review*, *Nimrod*, *New American Writing*, *North American Review*, *Witness*, *Verse Daily*, and the *Best Small Fictions Anthology 2022*. She has received nominations for the Pushcart Prize and awards from the Arts Foundation of Michigan, National Writer's Voice, Dyer-Ives Foundation, The Poetry Center (NJ), *Fish Anthology* (Ireland), and the Academy of American Poets. In 2023, she won first prize in the Allen Ginsberg Poetry Contest. The inaugural Poet Laureate of Grand Rapids, Michigan (2003–2005), Foster is the founder of the Contemporary Writers Series at Aquinas College.

www.ingramcontent.com/pod-product-compliance
Lightning Source LLC
Chambersburg PA
CBHW031446120626
46545CB00006B/2570